"All the President's Men and Women"

Bill Clinton
The 42nd President of the United States

Bob Italia

Published by Abdo & Daughters, 4940 Viking Drive, Suite 622, Edina, MN 55435.

Library bound edition distributed by Rockbottom Books, Pentagon Tower, P.O. Box 36036, Minneapolis, Minnesota 55435.

Cover Photo by: Black Star.
Inside Photos by: The Bettmann Archive (5, 7, 19, 21, 25, 27)
Wide World Photos, Inc. (6, 9, 20, 24)
Black Star (11, 15, 26)

Edited By Rosemary Wallner

Library of Congress Cataloging–in–Publication Data
Italia, Robert, 1955-
    Bill Clinton : the 42nd President of the United States / written by Bob Italia.
        p.   cm. — (All the President's men and women)
    Includes bibliographical references (p.) and index.
    Summary: Examines the life and political career of the man whose election as president in 1992 brought an end to twelve years of Republican rule.
    ISBN 1-56239-249-2
    1. Clinton, Bill, 1946- —Juvenile literature. 2. Presidents—United States—Juvenile literature. [1. Clinton, Bill, 1946- 2. Presidents.] I. Title. II. Series.
E886.I85   1993
973.929' 092—dc20   93-24849
[B]   CIP
                                                 AC

CONTENTS

A Time for Change

When Bill Clinton became governor of Arkansas in 1978, few people thought he would someday be president. After all, the 32-year-old politician gave little indication that he had set his sights on an even higher office.

But Clinton was ambitious. He had risen from humble origins to the governor's mansion through hard work and uncommon intelligence. Even when he was temporarily voted out of office in 1980, Clinton did not give up.

In 1992, his persistence paid off. The American economy was sluggish. People were out of work and in debt. The government seemed unable to do anything to help. The 46-year-old Clinton entered the race with promises of action. He defied early odds and defeated President George Bush. The stunning victory brought an end to 12 years of Republican rule, and set the stage for dramatic changes in America.

Hope

There was little in Clinton's early life that suggested he would one day attain greatness. William Jefferson (Bill) Clinton was born on August 19, 1946, in Hope, Arkansas. His father, William Blythe, had died in a car accident three months before Clinton's birth. Clinton's mother, Virginia, left him with her parents so she could go to New Orleans and become a certified nurse anesthetist.

President Bill Clinton speaks at the podium during his inaugural address, January 20, 1993.

Clinton's grandparents, Hardey and Mattie Hawkins, owned a grocery store outside of Hope. Clinton spent much of his time there. He also spent time with his aunts and uncles. One of Clinton's favorite was Uncle Buddy. He often told Clinton stories from which he learned many important lessons about life. Clinton called his uncle "the wisest man I ever met."

Clinton and his mother left Hope when he was four years old. They moved north to Hot Springs, but they often returned to Hope to visit relatives.

Battling Abuse

During one visit to Hope, Virginia met Roger Clinton, an automobile salesman. They soon married. Clinton was in Hope again—hoping for a normal, stable home life. But his stepfather had a drinking problem. Sometimes, he would get violent when he drank.

"I remember once when I was four or five and he actually fired a gun in the house," Clinton recalled. "There was a bullet hole in the wall. I had to live with that bullet hole, look at it every day." Roger was arrested and sent to jail.

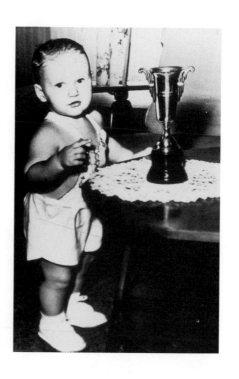

Bill Clinton as a toddler.

6

After the incident, the Clintons moved to Hot Springs for a new start. Roger worked as a service manager in his brother's Buick dealership. Virginia worked as a nurse anesthetist. When Clinton was ten years old, Roger and Virginia had a son, Roger, Jr.

The Clintons lived in a country house that did not have plumbing. But it was not a harsh life. "We were not poor," Clinton said. "A lot of rural Arkansas had no sewers back then."

Bill Clinton (left) with his mother, Virginia, and step-brother, Roger, in a 1959 family portrait.

Clinton attended a Catholic school in Hot Springs. Despite his father's continued drinking problem, Clinton excelled in his studies. He learned to live with his father's verbal and physical abuse. Clinton also learned that he had a natural talent for music. He went on to play saxophone for the Hot Springs High School Trojans band.

When Clinton was 14 years old, something happened that forever changed his life. Clinton decided to confront his stepfather and put an end to the violence that was tearing his family apart.

"I broke down the door of their room one night when they were having an encounter," Clinton recalled. "I told him that I was bigger than him now and there would never be any more of this while I was there."

Shortly afterward, his parents divorced. But only three months later, Roger convinced Virginia that he could reform. Clinton argued that Roger would never change. He tried to persuade his mother not to remarry him. But she did.

"She was old-fashioned and thought she must be to blame in some way," Clinton said of his mother. "She felt that [Clinton's half brother] Roger needed a father." The beatings did stop. In a show of family unity, 15-year-old Bill Blythe took his stepfather's surname and became Bill Clinton.

Bill Clinton: Musician

Clinton remained close to his mother, even though he and his brother were brought up by a maid who cared and cooked for them. The maid was religious, and hoped that Clinton would grow up to be a preacher.

"I was the most religious member of the family," Clinton admitted. "Mother got more religious later, as a result of the suffering she underwent."

President Clinton and Joe Henderson play their saxophones during the Arkansas Ball at the Washington Convention Center, Jan. 20, 1993.

Because his home life was so chaotic, Clinton became overly responsible in school and church. He raised funds and organized functions for charities. He also became the school band director's assistant for statewide planning. The band director, Virgil Spurlin, became Clinton's father figure.

Though others hoped Clinton would become a preacher, he secretly hoped to become a musician. He attended band camp every summer in the nearby Ozark mountains. He won first place in the state band's saxophone section. He also played in jazz combos. "He could sight-read with the best," said Spurlin. "And he kept me busy finding scores for him to read."

Clinton saw music as a way out of Hot Springs. Though he was an excellent student, Clinton received more music scholarships than academic ones when he graduated from high school.

The Political Calling

In 1956, the Clintons bought their first television set. Clinton saw the 1956 presidential campaigns and conventions and became fascinated with politics. As a class leader, Clinton was elected to Boys Nation. (Boys Nation is an American Legion-sponsored civics program.) In 1963, Clinton went to Washington as a delegate of Boys Nation to shake the hand of President John F. Kennedy in the White House.

The trip to Washington ended Clinton's dream of becoming a musician. Now, government and politics sparked his interest. Clinton asked his high school counselor to find him a college that offered a good program in foreign service. The only one she knew was Georgetown University.

Because Georgetown was in Washington, D.C., Clinton decided to attend. He ignored other suggestions from his counselor and did not even apply to other colleges.

Bill Clinton shakes hands with President John F. Kennedy at the White House (1963).

The acceptance period passed. The summer was half over. Clinton still had not heard from Georgetown. He did not know if the university had accepted him. But Clinton was not worried. He knew that the University of Arkansas in Fayetteville took any student with good grades. He could go to college there. Besides, Clinton had thought all along that he would be going to Arkansas. Clinton had become familiar with Fayetteville during his summers at band camps. And he wrote his junior paper about the university.

Eventually, Georgetown accepted Clinton. While working part time as an assistant to Arkansas Senator William Fullbright, Clinton earned a degree in foreign policy. In 1968, after his stepfather died of cancer, Clinton went to Oxford University in England as a Rhodes Scholar. There, he studied political science.

The Draft

In 1965, the Vietnam War began. Clinton opposed U.S. involvement in the war. He avoided the military draft by promising to attend a Reserve Officers Training Corps (ROTC) program at the University of Arkansas on his return from England. He wanted to go to Fayetteville because the law school was a good place to form political connections. His classmates and friends at Oxford knew he was ready to run for office.

But then Clinton briefly made himself eligible for the draft. He drew a high number in the selective service lottery. That meant he was unlikely to be drafted, since the low numbers were drafted first. Clinton returned to the U.S. in 1970 and enrolled in Yale Law School.

Hillary Rodham

Clinton met classmate Hillary Rodham at Yale. They began dating. In 1972, she joined Clinton in Texas. They worked together on Democrat George McGovern's unsuccessful campaign for presidency. Clinton was also a paid member of Gary Hart's staff. And Rodham was a vote registrar for the Democratic National Committee. Eventually, they fell in love.

At Yale, Clinton did not interview with law firms. "All I wanted to do was go home," he said. "I thought I would hang out my shingle in Hot Springs and see if I could run for office."

But the University of Arkansas needed new professors. After graduating from Yale in 1973, Clinton called the dean and discussed a teaching position. The dean said that Clinton was too young. Clinton responded, "Well, I'm that, but I'll teach anything you need for now, and I'm not interested in tenure, so I'll be no problem. It's a one-year deal." The dean agreed.

Clinton taught classes that no one wanted, such as admiralty law. He found teaching rewarding. He turned down an offer to be on the House staff for impeaching President Richard Nixon. Clinton tried to convinced Hillary Rodham to move to Arkansas. Rodham had accepted the offer to work on the impeachment staff that Clinton turned down. The two visited each other often, traveling back and forth between Washington and Fayetteville. They also spent long hours on the telephone.

The 1974 Congressional race approached. An Arkansas Congressman, John Paul Hammerschmidt, strongly supported Nixon. But Nixon was under fire for his involvement in the Watergate scandal.

Clinton was convinced that Hammerschmidt would suffer for backing Nixon. Clinton searched for a Democrat who would run against Hammerschmidt. When no one volunteered, Clinton decided to run himself.

No one gave him much of a chance. Hammerschmidt's district was devoutly Republican. Clinton was too young. He had a 1960s-style haircut, and his Yale and Oxford background was considered too liberal. But because of Watergate, Clinton ran surprisingly well against Hammerschmidt. Though Clinton did not win, he was encouraged to try again for a political office.

Hillary Rodham finally came to Arkansas to help with Clinton's next political campaign. She accepted an offer from the dean at the University of Arkansas to teach and run a legal clinic in Fayetteville. "I had no choice but to follow my heart there," Rodham said. "Following your heart is never wrong."

In 1975, Clinton and Rodham decided to marry Clinton bought a small house that his friends helped him paint just in time for the wedding. Friends considered the marriage a merger of "high talents." Both were intelligent and ambitious.

Rodham was not an ordinary young woman. On the night before the wedding, her mother asked to see the wedding dress. But Rodham had not bought one. Her mother convinced Rodham to go with her to the town square in Fayetteville. They found one store open, and Rodham bought the first dress she took from the rack. Her decision to keep her last name upset many of the state's conservatives.

President Clinton with his wife, Hillary, and daughter, Chelsea.

Governor Clinton

Clinton's campaign against Hammerschmidt gave him statewide attention. In 1976, he successfully campaigned for the attorney general position. He became well known as a consumer advocate. He fought utility rate hikes and pushed for stricter environmental controls.

In 1978, after one term as attorney general, Clinton was elected Arkansas' governor in 1978. At 32 years old, Clinton was the youngest sitting state chief executive in the country. He was also at the power center of the state.

But government power in Arkansas is limited. The legislature meets only twice a year for two months. To raise taxes, the law must be approved by three-quarters of the legislature. The office of governor has only a two-year term. And the governor's veto power is considered weak.

Clinton tried to build badly needed roads with new-car registration and license fees. This angered the state's small farmers, who buy new and used vehicles often. They would have to spend more money on these fees. Clinton also launched plans for the environment and schools. He brought in people from out of state. He also opposed clear-cut logging where all trees in a given area are cut down. And he raised school budgets by 40 percent. This offended a great number of people in Arkansas who weren't used to such dramatic changes. To them, Clinton seemed brash and arrogant.

After two years, Clinton was voted out of office. He was devastated. Only the birth of his daughter Chelsea that year softened the blow. It seemed that his political career was over.

But Clinton refused to give up. He reviewed his political mistakes. He started on a new plan to return to public office. He did what he knew best: He went out to talk to the people. This move won him many friends—and won him a new term as governor in 1982. Clinton made sure he won the support of other legislators before launching any new plans. He even sent his wife out to talk about education reforms.

Rodham had also undergone changes. She began to pay more attention to her appearance. She learned to talk in common terms with common people. And she also took her husband's surname. Hillary Rodham-Clinton was no longer an outsider. The education reforms passed—a major reason for Clinton's 12 successful years in office.

To accomplish this educational reform, Clinton had to rely on sales taxes. He knew that raising income taxes would only cause grumbling throughout the state. He had to cut corners and improvise. Sometimes he would accept offers to use corporate jets to get around the state. Otherwise, he could not go anywhere.

With his reforms, Clinton instilled a new sense of pride in the state. But he was not without his critics who called him "Slick Willie." They claimed he had given in to industry's wishes on controversial issues. But his supporters claim that Clinton is fair and compassionate.

In 1984, Clinton showed how fair and compassionate he could be. He approved a sting operation that led to the arrest of his half brother, Roger. Police had discovered that Roger was selling cocaine. Roger was jailed for a year. But Clinton helped him recover from drug and alcohol addiction by accompanying him to therapy sessions.

Running for President

In 1986, citizens rewarded Clinton for his hard work when the constitution was amended to give the governor a four-year term. By 1991, Clinton decided the time was right to run for President of the United States. The United States economy was sluggish. Clinton declared his candidacy on October 3, promising to "reinvent government."

Clinton was the early front runner. But then his campaign came to the brink of collapse. First, he was accused of being a womanizer. Then opponents questioned Clinton's story about how he avoided military service.

But Clinton showed his ability to take a blow and fight on. With sheer persistence, he captured the Democratic Party nomination on June 2, 1992. Clinton officially accepted the nomination on July 16 at the Democratic National Convention at Madison Square Garden in New York City.

*President Bill Clinton answers questions during a
"Town Meeting" broadcast from the studios of
WXYZ–TV in Southfield, Michigan.*

In his acceptance speech, Clinton spoke of family values. He told fathers who neglected their child support to take responsibility for their children. And he had a special message for children trying to grow up without a father or mother.

"I know how you feel," he said. "You're special, too. You matter to America. And don't you ever let anybody tell you you can't become whatever you want to be. And if other politicians make you feel like you're not a part of their family, come on and be part of ours."

Bill Clinton talks to young people during the taping of "An MTV Choose or Lose Special: Facing the Future With Bill Clinton" in Hollywood (June 1992).

Clinton also spoke of an ineffective, unfeeling government. He criticized President George Bush for lacking a "game plan." And he promised to create more jobs and improve education and health care. It was time for a change, he said. And the American people listened.

"In the name of all those who do the work, pay the taxes, raise the kids and play by the rules," he said, "in the name of the hard-working

President Clinton and Vice President Al Gore (second from right) head the pack, February 14, 1993, as they participate in the Run–for– Heart race in Washington, D.C.

Americans who make up our forgotten middle class, I proudly accept your nomination for the presidency of the United States."

The convention gave Bill Clinton a big boost. A few days later, when polls were taken, his popularity soared well past President Bush. To build on this growing popularity, the Clintons and the Gores campaigned across the country on a bus. They stopped in small towns, held meetings, and shook hands with everyone they could. Even after the Republican Convention in August, Clinton maintained the lead. When Independent candidate Ross Perot re-entered the race on October 1, Clinton's lead over Bush increased. By November 1, one major poll showed the following voter support: Clinton—44 percent, Bush—36 percent, Perot—14 percent.

Though he was well in the lead, Clinton did not rest. A relentless campaigner, Clinton campaiged as he did at the beginning. He spent the last 29 hours of his campaign in coffee shops and town halls, trying to shake every hand.

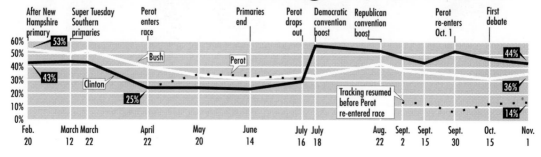

Election 1992: Tracking the Candidates

Election Day

On Election Day, Clinton returned to Little Rock. He voted at a community center with his wife and daughter. He waited in line with them, and when his turn came, he took Chelsea into the booth with him. When he emerged, he looked restless. Clinton knew what was about to happen.

The restlessness stayed with Clinton the remainder of the day. He was supposed to rest up for the night. But by early evening, he was jogging through downtown Little Rock, disregarding the rain.

Election '92: How the States Voted

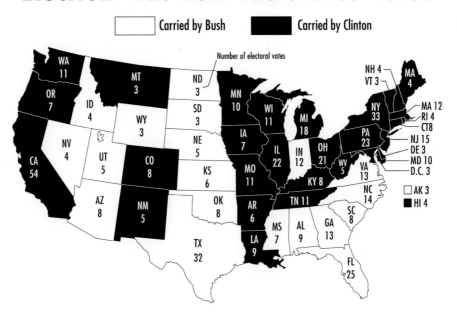

□ Carried by Bush   ■ Carried by Clinton

Clinton stopped at a McDonald's for a glass of water. All around him, people filled the downtown streets to watch the voter returns on giant outdoor screens. Most businesses had closed by 3 p.m. to make room for the celebration.

Bill Clinton visits a local McDonald's in downtown Little Rock.

The wind howled and the rain poured down, but people didn't seem to mind. They wandered about the streets of Little Rock, eating barbecue and drinking hot cider.

By nightfall, there was little suspense. The polls had been right all along. Bill Clinton won the election. He won 43 percent of the popular vote (Bush won 32 percent, Perot 18 percent), and 349 of 538 electoral votes.

The people of Little Rock cried and cheered. They danced in the streets. They hugged friends and strangers. And they held lighted candles in one hand, raised their other arm high, swayed, and sang "God Bless America" and "The Battle Hymn of the Republic."

When president-elect Bill Clinton finally appeared before them outside the Old State House, emotions soared. "My fellow Americans," he said as the people roared their approval. "I accept tonight the responsibility that you have given me to be the leader of this, the greatest country in human history. I accept it with a full heart and a joyous spirit."

One last time, Clinton spoke of change—the major theme of his campaign. And he promised to turn the country around. "We are all in this together," he said. "We will rise and fall together. Together, we

can make this country everything we want it to be." And then he
ended his speech with a tribute to the place where it all started. "I still
believe in a place called Hope."

A Chance for Greatness

Bill Clinton officially became the forty-second president of the United
States on January 20, 1993, at the inauguration ceremonies in

*President-elect Bill Clinton reaches out to the crowd gathered to greet
him after his acceptance speech, November 3, 1992, in
Little Rock, Arkansas.*

Washington, D.C. His stunning victory ended 12 years of Republican control of the White House, and renewed Democratic control of Congress.

But after all the celebrating was over, Clinton had a serious task ahead of him: He had to keep all his campaign promises. America was counting on change for the better. But how much would Clinton's reform plans cost? How could the deficit be reduced? And would the Republican-controlled Senate go along with those plans?

President Bill Clinton with his wife, Hillary, Vice President Al Gore and Tipper Gore at the Lincoln Memorial pre-inauguration gala, January 17, 1993.

Clinton has a wonderful opportunity before him. If he can turn the country around, Clinton may be remembered as one of the country's greatest presidents. But if he can't, we may see a Republican in the White House in less than four years.

As his wife Hillary looks on, Bill Clinton is sworn in by Chief Justice William Rehnquist as the 42nd U.S. President.

The Office of the President

When someone is elected President of the United States, that person takes on huge responsibilities. Presidents oversee laws passed by Congress. They are in charge of the armed forces. They also decide foreign policy—how America should help friendly nations and punish its enemies.

If the economy stumbles, the president must establish economic policies to help the country prosper. Presidents must make sure that laws are handed down fairly, that energy is used wisely, that children are educated, that citizens have jobs and are kept healthy.

No one person can possibly know everything there is to know to do a president's job. The president's main task is to set the country in the right direction. To help with the details, the president has a cabinet—a group of people he or she meets with regularly who advise the president on important decisions that must be made every day. The other books in this series detail some of the lives and duties of all the President's men and women.

Glossary

Campaign
A series of actions a person undertakes to attain a political goal.

Conservative
A person who opposes change.

Debate
A formal discussion or argument.

Deficit
The amount by which a sum of money falls short of the required amount.

Democrat
A member of the Democratic Party.

Economy
The management of a country's resources.

Independent
A person not associated with any established political party.

Liberal
A person favorable to progress and reforms.

Media

The means of mass communication, such as newspapers, magazines, radio, and television.

National Debt

The total financial obligations of a national government.

Petition

A formal, written request.

Political Parties

Political organizations, such as the Democratic and Republican parties.

Primary

A meeting of registered voters of a political party for the purpose of nominating candidates.

Republican

A member of the Republican Party.

Connect With Books

Almanac of American Presidents: From 1789 to the Present. Facts on File, 1991.

Beard, Charles Austin. *The Presidents in American History: George Washington to George Bush.* J. Messner, 1989.

Blassingame, Wyatt. *The Look-It-Up Book of Presidents.* Random House, 1990.

Degregorio, William A. *The Complete Book of U.S. Presidents: From George Washington to George Bush.* Barricade Books (New York), 1991.

Freidel, Frank. *The Presidents of the United States of America.* White House Historical Association, 1989.

Lengyel, Cornel Adam. *Presidents of the United States.* Golden Press, 1977.

Powers of the Presidency. *Congressional Quarterly,* 1989.

Index